But I Don't Know What To Say!

But I Don't Know What To Say!

Rebecca Wells

Rutledge Books, Inc.

Bethel, CT

Rutledge Books, Inc.
8 F.J. Clarke Circle, Bethel, CT 06801

Manufactured in the United States of America

Cataloging in Publication Data

Wells, Rebecca A.

But I don't know what to say! / Rebecca Wells.

p. cm.

ISBN 1-887750-53-3

1. Encouragement—Religious aspects—Christianity.

I. Title.

241.4—dc21 LC 97-65229

CIP

Dedication

I dedicate this book to our treasured grandchildren, Kaitlin, Gabriella, Matthew, Rebecca, Joshua, Christina and Mark, and any future additions God might have planned for us. Grandchildren are everything I was told they would be and more. Delivering joy into a bleak day, surprise when I least expect it, awesome honesty, energy at my most tired moments, tight hugs and warm smiles, they are, above all, great encouragers.

Acknowledgments

I'd like to thank the following people, whose support and encouragement have been soft, gentle nudges, moving me forward like a leaf blown by the wind.

Lionel (Chooch) Wells, my beloved husband, who has hesitantly watched me plunge with vigor into early retirement and writing. He desires retirement for himself, when at long last it arrives, to be a bit more relaxed. As my greatest encourager, he has read ceaseless manuscripts, and patiently waits his turn on our computer.

My children, Lori and her husband, Gary Smith; Todd and his wife, Elaine; Lynne and her husband, John Graziano; and Scott. They've plodded through more than their share of my publication attempts, offered great ideas, and encouraged me to keep trying. I love you.

My mother-in-law, Helen Wells, and other dear friends whose prayers were answered on October 1, 1973 — the day of my new birth in Christ. On that day, my husband got a new wife; our children a new mother; and God had a new kid in His kingdom. Just knowing what He did for me gives daily encouragement.

Dale Carnegie & Associates, Inc., sponsors of the Dale Carnegie course in Human Relations and the former

Dorothy Carnegie course, both of which I attended many years ago. These courses not only helped me overcome my fear of public speaking, but taught me much about relationships with people — of which encouragement is a great part.

My dear friends, Don and Verna Seibert. Don, unknown to him at the time, was instrumental to me in writing this book. His review and critique of the first complete draft gave valuable direction and much encouragement for the final rewrite.

My pastor, Steve McConnell, who constantly inspires and encourages me to serve God and to pursue writing efforts. His sermon, in which he related his story of a time when he didn't want to visit his very sick friend in the hospital, because he didn't know what to say, was indeed timely. I had just titled my book. What a confirmation!

My many friends from church and Bible study, who patiently read my early writings and kindly encouraged me to keep trying. I omit their names, because to leave out even one would be like missing a precious stone in a valuable piece of jewelry.

My God, who has blessed me with an abundance of talent in many areas of life, and energy to pursue those talents. His Son, my constant companion, Savior and Lord, is ever at my side.

Table Of Contents

Just Be There

How often, I ask, have you felt insecure
when needing to comfort a friend?
You'd like to encourage, and yet put aside
a task calling you to attend.

You stew and lament, making quite a great fuss,
along with excuses abundant,
convincing yourself any words you might say,
like those others say, are redundant.

I've been there myself, doing quite the same thing.
Discomfort creeps in like a worm.
It wiggles and jiggles, it wears and it tears, 'til like it,
I'm starting to squirm.

I've learned a great lesson that's worth passing on,
and, oh, what a diff'rence it makes.
When words pass you by, then encourage like this:
just be there...that's all that it takes.

Introduction

I sat behind a Christian brother and friend who had tenderly placed his right arm around his feeble, elderly mother-in-law's thin shoulders. Occasionally, with deep compassion, he looked down at her small face. I thought, *Jesus must have given that same compassionate look to those whose lives He touched*. Deeply moved, I returned home and wrote a note of encouragement to my friend.

I am a note writer. Frequently, after returning from church, I write notes to those who have moved me in some way that morning. Likewise, when I send cards to bereaved or troubled individuals, I include personal notes and scripture references. Yes, doing this takes time. Time, for each of us, is a precious commodity. When we share our time encouraging others, we give one of the greatest of all gifts.

Don't get the idea, however, that I never let an opportunity for encouragement slip by. I do. But I must admit that I like to receive notes and comments of encouragement—the golden rule applies here. To receive encouragement, I need to be an encourager. My purpose in writing this handbook is to build an army of encouragers whose friendly weapons are encouraging words.

Charles Swindoll, in his book *Encourage Me*, writes, "I know of no one more needed, more valuable, more *Christlike*, than the person who is committed to encouragement."[1] Having just completed reading Swindoll's book, already convicted that I must do more to encourage others, another event affirmed it. Donald Seibert, a committed Christian and former CEO of J.C. Penney Co., Inc., presently leads Sunday morning Adult Bible Study at my church. He mentioned at the close of one session that we all need to become encouragers — particularly by writing notes to others.

Returning home that morning, my thoughts continually focused on encouragement. *Why don't we do more of this*? I wondered. *We say we're too busy. We say we have no time. But perhaps it's because we're uncomfortable, especially when others are facing difficult times.*

Then the reason hit me like a dart hits the dartboard, and I believe it is on target: *We just don't know what to say.* None of us seem to have difficulty finding words of praise for accomplishments or special talents, which is also encouragement. Yet, we seem verbally paralyzed when it comes to encouraging those who are in the pits, struggling to pull themselves up.

As I began to read Christian counseling books, I compiled a list of the most frequent opportunities for encouragement, as I see them. My reading convinced me there is often a fine line between *offering encouragement* and *counseling*. Stepping over the line may be as natural as breathing. Offering upbeat scriptures and words to individuals can comfort, console, cheer and give assurance (encourage), as well as guide, instruct and perhaps correct (forms of counseling).

Counselors have specific credentials and are trained to accomplish their more difficult task, for more serious situations. Their role includes giving gentle reprimands. They require corrective action from those they counsel. If we find ourselves counseling, we should step back, remembering our purpose is to *build each other up*. An encourager need only be armed with sensitivity, compassion and loads of solid, positive comments.

The handbook that has resulted is purely from a lay person's point of view. No heavy theology impedes the reader. I trust it might help many of you to start new ministries. In whatever way you can, whether it be writing notes, making phone calls, or speaking face to face, *be an encourager*.

Be An Encourager

Be An Encourager:

Why Encourage Others?

Hebrews 3:13 sums it up: *"But encourage one another* daily, as long as it is called Today, *so that none of you may be hardened by sin's deceitfulness."* Every Christian is called to be an encourager — to say and do those things that will build our commitment level to Jesus Christ, while deepening our relationships with Him and others in our fellowship of believers.

Let's look at the last part of verse 13: ...*"so that none of you may be hardened by sin's deceitfulness."* We're all sinners. Separation from God, initiated by unconfessed sin, leads us down the path of deceitfulness — lying, cheating, deception, or dishonesty, to mention a few examples. This passage tells us that encouragement can keep believers from deceit. Encouragement is often the life raft at the side of a sinking ship...the rope that's lowered to pull a struggling person from deep, churning waters...the breath given by the CPR administrator. Encouragement is *life*.

A side benefit from encouraging others is the fantastic satisfaction in knowing we have cheered another up. Many persons will remember the time that you were there for them and remind you of that. But even if they don't, we feel blessed for having reached out to touch someone. An old Chinese proverb says, "A bit of fragrance always clings to the hand that gives you roses."

As we read Paul's writings, we note that he often opened or closed his epistles with encouraging words, as follows:

Opening: II Corinthians 1:1 Paul, an apostle of Christ Jesus by the will of God, and Timothy our brother, To the church of God in Corinth, together with all the saints throughout Achaia: 2 *Grace and peace to you* from God our Father and the Lord Jesus Christ. 3 Praise be to the God and Father of our Lord Jesus Christ, the Father of compassion and the God of all comfort, 4 *who comforts us in all our troubles, so that we can comfort those in any trouble with the comfort we ourselves have received from God.*

Closing: II Corinthians 13:11 Finally, brothers, good-by. *Aim for perfection, listen to my appeal, be of one mind, live in peace.* And the God of love and peace will be with you. 12 *Greet one another with a holy kiss.* 13 All the saints send their greetings. 14 May the grace of the Lord Jesus Christ, and the love of God, and the fellowship of the Holy Spirit be with you all.

Opening: Colossians 1:3 *We always thank God,* the Father of our Lord Jesus Christ, *when we pray for you,* 4 *because we have heard of your faith in Christ Jesus and of the love you have for all the saints—*

Closing: Colossians 4:17 Tell Archippus: "*See to it that you complete the work you have received in the Lord.*" 18 I, Paul, write this greeting in my own hand. *Remember my chains.* Grace be with you.

(In this example, Paul even encouraged the Colossians to pray for *him*, as he endured chains.)

Opening: Philippians 1:1 Paul and Timothy, servants of Christ Jesus, To all the saints in Christ Jesus at Philippi, together with the overseers and deacons: 2 Grace and peace to you from God our Father and the Lord Jesus Christ. 3 *I thank my God every time I remember you.* 4 In all my prayers for all of you, *I always pray with joy 5 because of your partnership in the gospel from the first day until now, 6 being confident of this, that he who began a good work in you will carry it on to completion until the day of Christ Jesus.*

Closing: Philippians 4:19 *And my God will meet all your needs according to his glorious riches in Christ Jesus.*

I like to envision us as Christian cheerleaders, encouraging our team of believers to give and do all that we are able, to grow in our faith, to increase our ability to cope with trials, to praise our Lord in all things, and to pass encouragement on to others. God's word is our encouragement. The more we study His word and the more deeply it is ingrained within us, the more naturally encouragement will occur. What a small price to pay to avoid becoming hardened by sin's deceitfulness.

Be An Encourager:

What Is Encouragement?

Ephesians 4:29 clarifies just what encouragement is and is not: "Do not let any unwholesome talk come out of your mouths, *but only what is helpful for building others up* according to their needs, that it may benefit those who listen." Simply stated, words that build others up are wholesome; those that offer criticism or tear others apart are unwholesome. Encouragers offer positive, upbeat, supportive words.

Encouragement ties in closely with Philippians 4:8-9, because what we *think* influences what we *say*. "Finally, brothers, whatever is true, whatever is noble, whatever is right, whatever is pure, whatever is lovely, whatever is admirable—if anything is excellent or praiseworthy—think about such things. Whatever you have learned or received or heard from me, or seen in me—put it into practice. And the God of peace will be with you."

Norman Vincent Peale taught persons around the globe to think positively, which is scriptural. Conditioning our minds to think good, wholesome thoughts is our best training to become encouragers. Positive, upbuilding words naturally come from the mouths of positive thinkers.

Let me stress a key ingredient of successful encouragement: *listening*. We should take every opportunity to *listen* before we speak. Sincere listening, with the heart as well as the ears, tells a person that we *truly care*. Listening with the heart is a very active process. If we hear only with our ears, we can't hear the underlying pain. I believe that when Jesus said, "He who has ears, let him hear," in Matthew 13:9 (NIV), He was speaking about understanding the *meaning* behind words. Listening with the heart is like being the good soil in the parable of the soils — good soil becomes productive.

Asking gentle questions that say, "tell me more," gives us an expanded view of the opportunity for encouragement. It verifies our interest. Speaking too soon, not understanding the real concern, can be like removing only one layer of wallpaper from a wall with several layers before putting up new paper or paint. When we don't get to the bottom, we're not on the real target.

Being a good listener is as much an art as speaking clearly and concisely. When we concentrate on words and meaning, we can't be thinking about what we are going to say. We listen to gain insight. Insight leads to wisdom when we speak. Above all, if someone trusts us with deep pain, let's keep all that we hear confidential.

Encouragement, like the first signs of spring, brings cheer and comfort; like a cool drink on a hot, summer day, it brings refreshment; like praise at the completion of a job well done, it brings reward; like the rainbow at the end of a storm, it brings hope; like a warm, loving hug during a time of grief, it brings consolation. Encouragement brings support and builds trust. It can turn pessimism to optimism.

Our willingness to offer encouragement to others can be the spark that ignites an attitude of encouragement in others. A tiny spark of sincere, warm encouragement might be all it takes to get others to pass it on.

Be An Encourager:

Who Is an Encourager?

All of us are called to be encouragers. Looking again at the words of Hebrews 3: 13, we read, "But encourage *one another* daily, as long as it is called Today..."Many persons think our ministers are the ones to whom this role has been assigned. Gratefully, I acknowledge the encouragement I constantly receive from my own ministers. Their weekly words of encouragement are like refreshing water to a parched, thirsty plant. Yet, our overworked ministers cannot possibly reach the vast number of persons in our communities who need encouragement. I Thessalonians 5:11 tells us this: "*Therefore encourage one another and build each other up*, just as in fact you are doing."

There is no place in scripture that says, "those of you who have the gift of encouragement, be an encourager." Although encouragement is listed as a gift from God in Romans 12:8, other scriptures indicate that all of us are to be encouragers. Each of us has daily opportunities to encourage others.

As parents and grandparents, we have a marvelous opportunity to challenge our children and grandchildren with encouragement. Just last week, one of my grandchildren was sitting at my side as I made a feeble attempt to handle a difficult part of a computer game. "You can do it, Grandma!" she cheered. Had someone not told her over and over again that *she* could do something, she would not have passed on the encouragement. We can build a world of encouragers of all ages.

As employees, we can change the atmosphere around us by becoming encouragers. Our companies will benefit from our uplifting and encouraging words — more work will get done and the attitude of the workplace will be improved, like adding thick, luscious icing to a plain cake. Surely God nods in approval at positive, upbuilding work environments.

As church leaders, committee chairpersons, choir members, and Sunday School teachers, we can bring glory to God while motivating those in our midst. Encouragement can cause the desire to give time and talents heartily as to the Lord to spring up like tiny mushrooms in moist, warm ground.

As spouses, we have the *privilege* of building each other up. As we work together around our homes, as we share our love in the presence of our children, we spread encouragement like soft butter on fresh bread. God smiles upon marriages and homes in which we cheer and comfort one another.

We must remember that performing the role of an encourager can be as draining as an onstage performance. Hopefully, encouragement will come back to us from others to renew our own energy level. Whatever our role in life may be, our script calls for encouragement.

Be An Encourager:

When Should We Encourage Others?

Again, looking at Hebrews 3:13, we read, "But encourage one another *daily*, as long as it is called Today..." God's people are in need of encouragement continually. The body of Christ, like most of our physical bodies, always hurts somewhere. Pain may be little, or extremely great, but it is perpetual.

There are times we all *need* encouragement, in addition to *giving* it. Perhaps we are not always honest with each other. We cover up our feelings in the same way that heavy makeup covers blemishes or masks conceal our physical identities. Oh, that we could uncover the flaws, the inconsistencies in our lives. Encouragement is needed from others to get us to open up, revealing when we have a need, a hurt, or a great pain.

Positive thinkers, in particular, fear sounding like complainers and often avoid sharing areas of hurt and concern. Putting on our cheerful, well-adjusted masks, we avoid letting others know the occasional painful realities in our lives. Sunday after Sunday, Christians sit in the pews listening to God's word, singing hymns, praying, and *greeting one another.*

"How are you today?" we ask one another.

"Just fine," we answer. Inside, we may be thinking, *That wasn't true at all. Why can't I just say that I'm really not doing so well...I'm anxious about my sister's emotional health...I'm deeply concerned about my father's financial situation and his health*...and on and on.

The church is not a building made of brick, wood or stone. The church is people — *real* people with *real* concerns, *every day*. The church comes together on Sunday, mixing together like our favorite stew ingredients mix together in a crock pot. We blend together for a couple of hours. At the end of the service or fellowship, the crock pot is unplugged and we go in all directions. If we don't let others know our needs when we're simmering together, we've lost a great opportunity for support once we've left there. But more importantly, we've denied another the opportunity to become an encourager.

Although opportunities to encourage one another seem natural within our churches, where we are more accustomed to confessing faults and concerns, opportunities abundantly flourish elsewhere.

- Neighbors face crises daily. Kind, uplifting words bring a soothing balm. A homemade pie or cake converts the balm to a great edible treat.
- Our children occasionally come home from school discouraged after tests, trials, or unsatisfying performances in athletic events. Hugs, kind words, and homemade cookies say, "I love you anyway, just the way you are."
- Our spouses are stressed at the office or workplace, needing cheer when they arrive home. Placing a fresh picked rose in the center of the table, preparing a favorite dessert, or just taking time to listen can offer consolation.
- A grocery store clerk, perhaps having a bad day, appears disgruntled as she scans our order. Saying "You're doing a great job — thanks," can bring more than a smile. The next customer may get faster service.
- A gas station attendant (for those of us who don't

self-serve) tiredly drags his feet as he moves from pump to car. Making eye contact as we pay, along with our sincere words, "Have a good day," can be uplifting.

• Frustration upon a young mother's face reflects the loud, distracting cries of her baby. Letting her know that these difficult days will pass quickly can give her hope.

• An elderly person struggles with a walker. "Let me hold the door for you" may seem trite to you, but immensely helpful to the one struggling.

There's nothing extraordinary about the situations I've mentioned. They are *ordinary*—that's the point. Such opportunities for encouragement face each of us daily.

Encouragement doesn't always require words.

• As a person overloaded with packages drops an item, we can pick it up and hand it to them.

• A free smile given to another who waits in the doctor's office can be almost as good as costly medicine.

• A touch to the shoulder of one who is weighed down with cares can say more than many words.

• The person in the check-out line before us, searching for a couple of pennies, is relieved and cheered when we offer our own.

• Fresh baked goods set out for the repairman or construction worker brings delight and, perhaps, better service.

Sometimes just *being there* with nothing to offer but ourselves brings consolation.

• A warm hug for the one who has just lost a mate of many years says we are there and we *care*. Words can come later.

• A meal taken to one who has suffered illness lifts spirits and fills a need, even when we don't stay to talk.

• The words, "I'll be right over," bring hope, even when we're convinced the necessary words aren't going with us. Being there will suffice.

Actions alone, driven by compassion and empathy, can silently build up one another. 'Tis far better to be there with a wordless hug than to not be there at all. Encouragement doesn't have to be audible.

Be An Encourager:

Where Should We Offer Encouragement?

In the *who* section, I mentioned situations in which all of us can be encouragers. The *when* section amplifies examples of encouragement. *Wherever* we are each day of our lives is our particular place to bring encouragement.

Bruce Larson, in his book, Wind and Fire, *points out some interesting facts about sandhill cranes: "These large birds, who fly great distances across continents, have three remarkable qualities. First, they rotate leadership. No one bird stays out in front all the time. Second, they choose leaders who can handle turbulence. And then, all during the time one bird is leading, the rest are honking their affirmation. That's not a bad model for the church. Certainly we need leaders who can handle turbulence and who are aware that leadership ought to be shared. But most of all, we need a church where we are all honking encouragement."* [2]

We are likely to think first of the church as a place where we can honk encouragement. Let's remember *we are the church in the world.* We bring the love of Jesus Christ wherever we go, because His Spirit lives within us. You've heard it said that often we are the only Bible someone will read. What others see in us might possibly lead them to seek Him in their lives. Encourage one another daily, wherever we are.

Be An Encourager:

How Can We Encourage Others?

Although I hope this handbook will generate encouragment using various methods at *all times*, and in *all situations*, I encourage everyone to *write encouraging notes* to one another. I feel sad that writing has become almost out of style. Our busy lives have pushed that skill and desire into a dark corner where dust and dirt have embedded it to oblivion. Although it is easy to type a quick note and push the "send" button on E-mail, handwritten notes carry far more love and warmth.

Written encouragement can be held onto, to be read over and over again. Many of us are more open when we write. Words that get stuck in our throats while speaking find their way onto a piece of paper with greater ease. Feelings deep within our hearts can be graciously poured out like warm coffee from the urn when we sit in a quiet place, reflecting upon the one to whom we write.

Sunday after Sunday, we hear prayer requests during our worship services. As members of prayer chains, we are reminded daily of needs that exist. We read of neighbors, friends, and even those we don't know in our community who are suffering some kind of pain.

The following pages of this book list opportunities for encouragement in situations that cause concern. Let it be noted, however, although my emphasis is upon situations that are discouraging or upsetting — i.e., *concerns*, it is not my intent that we solely focus our encouragement upon these.

Persons who are blessing others with their talents, time, and abilities deserve encouragement in the same way. Persons who are experiencing great joys in life also deserve words of encouragement and praise. Lack of encouragement at these times can, in itself, become discouraging to individuals. Personally, I find encouragement much easier in those situations, and have chosen not to elaborate upon them.

To encouragers, writing *and* speaking, I have *provided*:

1) an encapsulated, limited description of each *opportunity for encouragement* — my layperson's view
2) scriptures that focus upon each particular situation
3) words to say — to share, and
4) words to pray — specific prayer inclusions.

If you choose to write notes, I would suggest using either a general "thinking of you" type of card and adding a personal, handwritten note of encouragement, or simply taking a blank note card and writing the appropriate sentiment. Each of us will develop our own style, the more notes we write. Additionally, the more we write, the easier it becomes to *speak* the language of encouragement.

Begin your note by stating a positive, upbuilding quality of the person to whom you are writing. Briefly share your awareness of their concern, and offer one of the suggested scriptures, or one of your own. My selections are surely not all inclusive, nor is the entire scripture necessary in all cases.

Add one or more of the "words to say," as written, or in your own words. Close the note with a short prayer, similar to those at the close of devotionals, or write, "I will be praying that..."

Allow me to share an example letter, taking the opportunity to encourage one who is anxious.

Dear Sally,

Thank you for sharing with me your anxiety over present job concerns. I am grateful to be your friend and count it a privilege to pray for you. I'm probably one of the worst when it comes to worry — I'm one of those persons who can make mountains out of molehills.

When I am anxious about something, I find Philippians 4:6 to be of great help. "Do not be anxious about anything, but in everything, by prayer and petition, with thanksgiving, present your requests to God." Someone told me that it helps to ask what is the worst thing that can happen. Usually, the worst is not that bad.

I'll be praying that you can turn your cares over to God and rest in the assurance that He will indeed meet all your needs. If I can be of any help, I am here for you.

Love,
Becky

This same pattern can be followed in a telephone conversation, allowing for responses and reactions from the other person. We encourage each other because we love each other. Perfect love casts out fear, depression, discouragement, resentment and other stressful experiences. Let's build each other up, starting now.

Opportunity For Encouragement

Opportunity For Encouragement

Marital Difficulties

My husband and I stood before God, our minister, friends, and family many years ago and recited our marriage vows. A *wedding* took place on that day; yet, our *marriage* takes place daily. God created marriage with the desire and intent that He be invited to the center spot. God is the One who turns a marriage into holy matrimony.

My husband and I were not trained for marriage in the sense that we were trained for careers. For years, we stumbled our way through it, like short-legged persons in a jungle of heavy brush. Fortunately, we were committed to the vows we made and pushed onward. Great times awaited us when we came to clearings; struggles took over when the brush became dense. Perhaps our greatest lack was good communication. Entangled, and caught up in our own problems, we didn't really hear what the other was saying.

Attending a Marriage Encounter weekend changed our marriage and led us to a ministry with that organization. Thinking that we knew each other well after almost twenty-four years, we went on the weekend not expecting any new revelations. We discovered that we had been *competing* with each other, head-butting, rather than working in relationship with each other as the helpmate

God intended. It was also eye-opening for us to learn that when we are out of relationship with each other, we are out of relationship with God.

Many years earlier, I read that concept in the book, *Miracle in Darien*, by Bob Slosser. At that time, the meaning had floated only on the surface of my being, like oil on water, and did not sink in. Quoting Terry Fullam, Bob wrote, "The fact of the matter is — now here's the point, don't miss it — *our horizontal relationships with one another have been made by God to be the test of our vertical relationship with Him.*"[3] This truth is applicable to all our relationships.

Commitment is not easy — it calls for work from each partner. There must be mutual respect. Successful communication skills are critical. Each person must be willing to give time and effort to work at making the marriage all that God desires. Above all, there must be spiritual unity. Couples whose marriages are a threesome, with God at the center, who study God's word, and pray together, stay together.

When we become aware of other's struggles in a marital relationship, it's helpful if our own marriage is solid. It's tough to encourage those in a hard place if we're stuck there ourselves. Marriage seems to be the area most under spiritual attack these days. I encourage every reader to study and read good books on marriage in an effort to strengthen our own relationships. Reading and studying God's plan for our marriages prepares us to help others.

Attendance at Christian-based marriage seminars and conferences is one of the best gifts we can give ourselves. And a great marriage is absolutely the *best gift* we can give our children. Their prime example is that which they see every day, living before their eyes.

We can likewise encourage those outside our families

by the example we set in our own marriage. Many churches are offering marriage mentor programs, in which couples with great marriages offer to mentor a young married couple. What an encouragement!

Serious marital difficulties most often require a counselor. The Marriage Encounter Weekend is not recommended for couples who have serious problems or are undergoing psychological counseling. Couples in that situation have attended, often as a last ditch effort, after trying everything else. Many have found the key to open new discoveries about each other and their relationship. Others have not.

Unless our friendship with another couple is extremely close and we know the degree to which problems exist, sensitivity is an absolute must in offering anything other than general encouragement. We need to remember, however, when friends are going through serious marital difficulties, beyond our scope of helping, we can still be there offering our love and compassion, along with upbeat, kind words. Just because we're not trained counselors doesn't mean we should walk away.

Peter Marshall wisely said:

We are souls living in bodies. Therefore when we really fall in love, it isn't just physical attraction. If it is just that, it won't last. Ideally, it's also spiritual attraction. God has opened our eyes and let us see into someone's soul. We have fallen in love with the inner person, the person who is going to live forever. That's why God is the greatest asset to romance. He thought it up in the first place. Include him in every part of your marriage, and he will lift it above the level of the mundane to something rare and beautiful and lasting.[2]

Suggested inclusions for letters, notes, and conversations:

Scriptures

Ephesians 5:33

However, each one of you also must love his wife as he loves himself, and the wife must respect her husband.

Ephesians 4:26

"In your anger do not sin" : Do not let the sun go down while you are still angry...

Ephesians 4:32

Be kind and compassionate to one another, forgiving each other, just as in Christ God forgave you.

Matthew 19:4-6

4 "Haven't you read," he replied, "that at the beginning the Creator 'made them male and female,' 5 and said, 'For this reason a man will leave his father and mother and be united to his wife, and the two will become one flesh'?
6 So they are no longer two, but one. Therefore what God has joined together, let man not separate."

I Corinthians 7:3-4

3 The husband should fulfill his marital duty to his wife, and likewise the wife to her husband. 4 The wife's body does not belong to her alone but also to her husband. In the same way, the husband's body does not belong to him alone but also to his wife.

I Peter 3:7

> Husbands, in the same way be considerate as you live with your wives, and treat them with respect as the weaker partner and as heirs with you of the gracious gift of life, so that nothing will hinder your prayers.

Words to say

- How about the two of you coming over for dinner?
- I love you both and want you to know that.
- Something special attracted you to each other. What was it?
- After we find the right mate, we must *be* the right mate.
- Schedule a date night just to talk.
- Our challenge is to keep respect alive, even if love appears dead.
- We all struggle with forgiving and *forgetting*.
- Be supportive and encouraging to your spouse.
- Try listening with your heart as well as your ears.
- Read the scriptures concerning marriage—over and over.
- If possible, do things *together*—especially in your church.

- Reach out and touch each other often.

- Praise God *in* everything you go through, not *for* everything.

- You can decide to love your spouse, even when you don't feel like it.

Words to pray — if you want to close your letter or conversation with a prayer, you might include:

- Prayer that the couple will ask God to be the center of their marriage.

- Asking that God will give each person respect for the other.

- Prayer that God will show the couple His plan for their lives.

- Prayer that God will give the couple an understanding of their commitment.

- Praise to God for bringing this couple together.

- Prayer that the couple will learn to listen to one another with their hearts.

- Prayer that God would renew the couple's love for each other.

Opportunity For Encouragement:

The Need For Patience

Hurry, hurry, hurry! We hear it. We say it. This fast-paced age seems to *demand* it. Our nerves get as taut as newly tuned piano strings, waiting to snap with one more tug. We know what God desires for us, based on I Corinthians 13:4-5 — "Love is patient, love is kind... it is not easily angered..."

Patience, a fruit of the spirit, (Galations 5:22) is one of the characteristics that Christians are supposed to possess, yet one that few persons, including Christians, possess to the degree we should. A patient person is somewhat like a sponge — soft, flexible, and able to absorb strain and stress without much reaction. Inconveniences that disrupt the life of a patient person create very little disturbance — they just soak in.

Impatient persons, on the other hand, tend to be like chunks of inflexible paraffin. Lacking flexibility, they can't bend to allow something unplanned into their structure. Words of encouragement, applied over time, can be the warmth that softens them to a more pliable state. This may be a "little by little" process, and we must remain patient. As we encourage persons exhibiting impatience, we can be confident that our words will eventually soften our target.

Patience comes in different sizes and strengths,

somewhat like pain killers. We're all tested in little day to day situations that require the "quick, grab it now and use it" kind that helps us to maintain daily sanity. In addition, some patience must be "longer and stronger," equaling a double, triple, or greater dose. Long-suffering, steadfastness, forbearance, endurance — all these terms remind us of the greater opportunity to exhibit patience in our lives. As we practice it, it will rub off.

God allows trials and suffering that tests our patience to come our way for a reason: *to build our character.* Eventually, if we are maturing in our faith, we'll see beneficial results from trials, either major or less significant. Perhaps the reason trials produce character is because God has promised to go through them with us. As He walks closely beside us, or even carries us through the desert, some of His patience rubs off. When we're feeling impatient, it helps to remember His patience with us.

Read the following tribute to a minister who exhibited patience:

In his book The Uttermost Star, *F.W. Boreham told about attending a farewell service for a minister who was leaving a church he had pastored for 20 years. Several preachers attended, and each eloquently extolled the pastor's virtues. Boreham commented that he had forgotten everything said that day except for a simple statement made by a man who was not even scheduled to speak. The man had asked permission to say a word, and in a single sentence had paid his pastor this compliment, "I have seen him nearly every day of my life for 20 years, and I've never seen him in a hurry!" After the service, the minister said he considered that tribute to be the most gratifying. He took it as an indication that over the years he had truly learned to wait patiently upon the Lord.* [2]

Suggested inclusions for letters, notes, and conversations:

Scriptures

I Corinthians 13: 4-5

4 Love is patient, love is kind. It does not envy, it
does not boast, it is not proud.
5 It is not rude, it is not self-seeking, it is not easily
angered, it keeps no record of wrongs.

Galatians 5:22-23

22 But the fruit of the Spirit is love, joy, peace,
patience, kindness, goodness, faithfulness,
23 gentleness and self-control. Against such things
there is no law.

James 5:8-9

8 You too, be patient and stand firm, because the
Lord's coming is near.
9 Don't grumble against each other, brothers, or
you will be judged. The Judge is standing at the
door!

Romans 5:3-5

3 Not only so, but we also rejoice in our sufferings,
because we know that suffering produces perseverance;
4 perseverance, character; and character, hope.
5 And hope does not disappoint us, because God
has poured out his love into our hearts by the Holy
Spirit, whom he has given us.

Philippians 4:11

I am not saying this because I am in need, for I have learned to be content whatever the circumstances.

Psalm 37:7

> Be still before the LORD and wait patiently for him; do not fret when men succeed in their ways, when they carry out their wicked schemes.

Words to say

- Focus only on the task at hand.
- Little disruptions offer big opportunities to grow.
- God doesn't expect us to do more than we can or be more than we can.
- I liked your reaction to that situation. Keep it up.
- The more we get done, the more there is to do.
- Take a deep breath — count to ten — smile.
- Noah Webster spent 36 years on his dictionary.
- Sometimes I think our patient God must chuckle at our impatience.
- Patience, like athletics, requires training.
- If you're as patient as you want to be, you have no room to grow.
- Live one day at a time; what doesn't get done today waits for tomorrow.
- God isn't finished with any of us yet.

- What is the worst that can happen if something doesn't get done today?

- We might feel better when we explode, but others don't.

Words to pray — if you want to close your letter or conversation with a prayer, you might include:

- Prayer that God will put within the person a desire to cultivate patience.

- Prayer that God will make the person sensitive to areas in which he/she needs patience.

- Prayer that the person will try to identify those things that trigger impatience.

- Prayer that the person will be open to God's gentle reminders of the need for patience.

- Thank God that there is hope for those with the indwelling Spirit of Christ.

- Praise to God that He will help us to be overcomers in this area.

Opportunity For Encouragement:

Indecision

We've all been there...standing at a crossroad in life, desperately seeking guidance for direction. Either road could lead to a wonderful place. Although it's not always a case of one road being right and one being wrong, we're confident that one will be *better* for us at this point in time. The best road is the one that follows God's will.

As Christians, we believe that God has a plan for our lives. He already knows every decision we will make as we stand at each crossroad. Of course, He could make His plan as obvious as snowflakes on a black pavement, but we would miss a wonderful opportunity to grow spiritually. Missing the opportunity to seek His will, we would miss the opportunity to know Him better.

As we seek the will of God in making a decision, we may get clear guidance...a scripture that repeatedly comes to us, words from a person we trust and love, God's incidences that take place. On the contrary, we may receive no confirmation regarding our planned direction. One thing is sure: God gives us peace when we are living according to His will. We can confidently assure others of this.

Before we seek the will of God in making a decision, we should be sure we *want to do His will*. Clear guidance might come, revealing we are to make a decision we don't prefer. Sometimes the door closes on what *we* want or prefer. Believing that God closed one door and is opening another for our sake is important to our peace of mind. Whatever we do, after we make the decision, we should avoid asking "what if I had done something else?"

The following story holds much wisdom:

Recently my husband was faced with a decision affecting his career and our way of life as a family. Making the decision was agony, and when it was made we were still tormented by doubts. Then a dear friend passed on to us some words that had been given to her husband years ago by a former president of Bowdoin College. When a decision has been made and the die is cast, then, said this wise gentleman, murder the alternatives. - Mrs. Emory S. Adams, Jr. [2]

Suggested inclusions for letters, notes, and conversations:

Scriptures

Proverbs 3:5-6

5 Trust in the LORD with all your heart and lean not on your own understanding;
6 in all your ways acknowledge him, and he will make your paths straight.

Matthew 6:33

But seek first his kingdom and his righteousness, and all these things will be given to you as well.

Proverbs 12:2

All a man's ways seem right to him, but the LORD weighs the heart.

James 3:17

But the wisdom that comes from heaven is first of all pure; then peace-loving, considerate, submissive, full of mercy and good fruit, impartial and sincere.

Psalm 40:8

"I desire to do your will, O my God; your law is within my heart."

Words to say

- If we honestly seek God's will, He will make His plan known to us.
- We'll make some bad decisions and some good ones. The important thing is to *make* them.
- The more decisions we make, the better we get!
- Expect God to open or close doors.
- Expect God to bring peace to your heart.
- If your decision agrees with the Bible, if there is peace, if circumstances agree, it is most likely the right decision.
- Take your time; often the answer doesn't come immediately.
- Ask yourself if you are willing to do what God wants.

- Weigh all the facts, then make the decision.

- Second guesses are off limits.

- Once you make a decision, forget it.

Words to pray — if you want to close your letter or conversation with a prayer, you might include:

- Praise to God for the knowledge that He will reveal His plan to the person.

- Prayer for wisdom in decision making.

- Prayer for patience during the decision making process.

- Prayer that the person will receive a confirmation regarding the decision.

- Prayer that the person will have peace in his/her heart after making the decision.

Opportunity For Encouragement:
Low Self-Worth

Our particular area in New Jersey received approximately eighty inches of snow this winter — eighty inches of snowflakes, each unique. Is that mind-boggling? As each flake was packed to the ground with the weight of new falling snow, perhaps some of its uniqueness disappeared. Yet, we can be sure each was unique when it first fell.

On the heels of winter came a lovely assortment of flowers and flowering bushes to brighten our daily lives. Again, no two were exactly alike, although our eyes can't distinguish the differences. Creator God makes all things new and different.

Including you. You are as unique as a snowflake or beauteous flower. God has given you abilities, talents, characteristics and a physical form unlike that of any other person alive. You might have a laugh that is contagious, a smile that warms the heart of anyone who receives it, a gentle touch that immediately lets another know your love, a voice that is soft and silky.

You might be able to sing beautifully, to write wonderful poetry, to read aloud with great expression, to manage a budget and balance a checkbook without difficulty, to exhibit great physical stamina. Each of us has something or things we can do well. Some of us take longer than others to open the package and discover what our unique gifts are.

During times of stress or discouragement, we might forget how very special God has created us to be. At those times we should recall His words to us, from Psalm 139..."You knit me together in my mother's womb" (v.13)..."I am fearfully and wonderfully made" (v 14)..."My frame was not hidden from You when I was made in the secret place." (v. 15)

God has a plan and purpose for each of us. Sometimes that plan allows us, even mandates us, to go through difficult times, during which we might question our self-worth. It's normal. At such times, we can *be overcomers* or *be overcome.* God chooses us to be overcomers, because He cares so very much about each of us, all the time, in whatever situation we find ourselves.

Our God wants to rebuild us when we've been shattered, to renew us when we've become flawed, to uplift us when quicksand pulls us down, to sustain us when strength is zapped, to encourage us when we're down. Sometimes, however, just when we think we know what He wants us to be, and we're feeling pretty good about ourselves, He surprises us.

Read this story of The Potter's Hammer:

A visitor to the shop of a famous potter was puzzled by one operation which seemed to have little purpose. The workman was beating a lump of clay with a large mallet. It looked as if nothing was happening, and so the one who was taking the tour finally asked, "Sir, why are you doing that?"

"Just wait and watch the results; then you'll understand," was the reply.

He heeded the advice and soon noted that the top of the mass began to quiver and swell as little bumps formed on its surface. "Now you can see the need for the pounding," said the man. "I could never shape the clay into a worthwhile vessel if these bubbles remained in it, so I must gradually work them out."

The one watching was a Christian and immediately recalled the 18th chapter of Jeremiah. He saw more clearly than ever before why the great Potter must work upon our souls. The discipline of chastening and the trials God sends are necessary to eliminate pride and self-will. This is the only way the Master can form us into beautiful vessels capable of holding the treasures of His grace.[2]

Suggested inclusions for letters, notes, and conversations:

Scriptures

Psalm 139:13

For you created my inmost being; you knit me together in my mother's womb.

Psalm 139:16

...your eyes saw my unformed body. All the days ordained for me were written in your book before one of them came to be.

Psalm 8:4-5

4...what is man that you are mindful of him, the son of man that you care for him?
5 You made him a little lower than the heavenly beings and crowned him with glory and honor.

Isaiah 43:7

...everyone who is called by my name, whom I created for my glory, whom I formed and made."

Ephesians 2:10

For we are God's workmanship, created in Christ

Jesus to do good works, which God prepared in advance for us to do.

Ephesians 4:24

...and to put on the new self, created to be like God in true righteousness and holiness.

I Timothy 4:4

For everything God created is good, and nothing is to be rejected if it is received with thanksgiving,

James 1:18

He chose to give us birth through the word of truth, that we might be a kind of firstfruits of all he created.

Words to say

- God loves you just the way you are.
- God loves you so much, He knows the number of hairs on your head.
- You're someone special—you're the only one of your kind.
- Even tarnished gold can be polished like new.
- God doesn't make mistakes. He knew what He was doing when He created you.
- Play a King David role. Ask yourself, "Why am I cast down?"
- We're usually harder on ourselves than on others.

- Write down all the things you like and dislike about yourself. What can you do to put more things in the "like" column?

- If we concentrate on our strong points, the weak ones will diminish.

- God wants the best for you.

Words to pray — if you want to close your letter or conversation with a prayer, you might include:

- Prayer that the person will see the good in him/herself.

- Praise to God for making this person wonderfully unique.

- Prayer that the person will use his/her God given talents to build His kingdom.

- Prayer that if change is necessary, the person might sincerely desire it.

Opportunity For Encouragement:

Anxiety, Worry, Tension (Stress)

"Don't make mountains out of molehills!" Has anyone ever said that to you? If so, you were probably worrying. Unfounded fears about what might happen can consume so much of our time that we forget to live in the present. We can become nervous, sleepless, and even have difficulty breathing. For many persons, the anxiety and worry leads to nervous breakdowns. Yet, we are told that the biggest percentage of things we worry about never come to pass.

Modern terminology refers to anxiety, worry, and tension as stress. None of us achieve freedom from it; yet, it is one of the most destructive forces we face. For Christians, the solution to stress is basically simple, yet difficult to achieve. I Peter 5: 7 tells us to cast all our anxieties on Him for He cares about us. It's as simple as writing the concern on a piece of paper and handing it to a friend. Because, after all, He is our best friend. Our human nature, however, encourages us to lean upon ourselves and our own understanding. We listen to the active, pesty little voice saying, "Worry your way through this!"

Problems causing stress can be real or imagined. Either kind can lead us to have pity parties that get in the way of the solution. God wants us to be free from stress; He wants to shoulder all our concerns. As we study the Word of God and learn to praise Him in all situations, we become victors over stress.

We can encourage one another to practice praise and prayer regularly, replacing anxiety and worry with positive thoughts. When anxiety tries to creep in like a thief in the night, we can rely on our greatest security system, God, to take over if we'll let Him. We can rest in Him.

According to the National Bureau of Standards, a dense fog covering seven city blocks to a depth of 100 feet is composed of something less than one glass of water. That is, all the fog covering seven city blocks 100 feet deep could be, if it were gotten all together, held in a single drinking glass; it would not quite fill it.

This can be compared to the things we worry about. If we could see into the future and if we could see our problems in their true light, they wouldn't blind us to the world — to living itself — but instead could be relegated to their true size and place. And if all the things most people worry about were reduced to their true size, you could probably stick them all into a water glass, too.[2]

It's important to realize the difference between *planning* for tomorrow and *worrying* about tomorrow. Planning represents time well spent — thinking and praying about goals and schedules, trusting God to lead. Planning for tomorrow, asking God to lead, can actually help reduce worry. Worrying about tomorrow takes God's leadership away.

Suggested inclusions for letters, notes, and conversations:

Scriptures

I Peter 5:7

Cast all your anxiety on him because he cares for you.

Psalm 94:19

When anxiety was great within me, your consolation brought joy to my soul.

James 1:2-3

Consider it pure joy, my brothers, whenever you face trials of many kinds, because you know that the testing of your faith develops perseverance.

Psalm 56:9

Then my enemies will turn back when I call for help. By this I will know that God is for me.

I Thessalonians 5:18

give thanks in all circumstances, for this is God's will for you in Christ Jesus.

Romans 8:28

And we know that in all things God works for the good of those who love him, who have been called according to his purpose.

Matthew 6:34

Therefore do not worry about tomorrow, for tomorrow will worry about itself. Each day has enough trouble of its own.

Psalm 42:5

Why are you downcast, O my soul? Why so disturbed within me? Put your hope in God, for I will yet praise him...

Philippians 4:6-7

6 Do not be anxious about anything, but in everything, by prayer and petition, with thanksgiving, present your requests to God.
7 And the peace of God, which transcends all understanding, will guard your hearts and your minds in Christ Jesus.

Words to say

- Plan ahead.
- Be realistic in your plans and goals.
- There's always tomorrow.
- God is in control of everything.
- Practice an attitude of gratitude continually.
- The worst thing that can happen probably isn't so bad.
- Pretend you are putting all your cares in a bundle; then picture yourself laying them at the foot of Jesus. He'll handle them.
- Live one day at a time.
- The God who gave you life will take care of you.

- If you can keep your mind on Christ, you'll find more peace.

- Remember that very few things we worry about ever happen.

Words to pray — if you want to close your letter or conversation with a prayer, you might include:

- Gratitude that He will take all the person's concerns.

- Prayer for complete peace of God for the person.

- Praise for Him who hears the prayers of two or more persons gathered in His name.

- Praise that God's word is true, and that we can believe Him.

Opportunity For Encouragement:

Illness

Illness afflicts us in many ways...small, big, painful, ugly, external, internal, short-lived, and permanent, to name a few. Whether a headache or a serious infliction, illness keeps us from being the person we'd like to be. It wedges into our lives like an unwanted thorn into a finger. Minor headaches affect our disposition; major handicaps might affect our security and confidence. Illness, like a mask, often conceals our true selves.

Illness impacts everyone. Sometimes we know the cause: we ate too much, or the wrong kind of foods...had caffeine when we knew better...wore shoes that were not the best for us...inherited a physical condition.

Sometimes the cause of our illness is unknown, evasive even to doctors. Occasionally, the cause is deep sin in our lives, hiding like a spider at the outside of its web, waiting for something to alert it. Yet, we refuse to admit what is tugging at us, causing ongoing discomfort and pain. Often, persons hold on to sin, despite strong suspicion that it may be causing illness. How much better it would be to confess the sin and get on with healthy, wholesome life.

Illness and infirmities are difficult for us to accept and admit. We often equate them with weakness instead of viewing them as the route to strength. Persons who know us well may be totally unaware of our secret pain. Others can't encourage us when we take this approach. Likewise, we miss opportunities to encourage others who are just like us.

God often allows persons to suffer great infirmities and uses them mightily as servants, as in the case of Joni Eareckson Tada. Her diving accident as a teenager left her a quadriplegic who brings glory to God with the dynamic ministry He's given her. Joni's radio program cheers me up daily. When she sings, her voice is strong, soothing and *whole.* If you didn't know otherwise, you couldn't tell her angelic voice is being projected from a wheelchair.

Much physical suffering has been used through the ages to bring glory to God. It's a fact that sometimes God chooses to heal, and sometimes He has other plans that will bring greater glory to His kingdom. Our great assurance comes in knowing that we'll all be healed one day... given heavenly new bodies. Our great physician will change us in a moment of time.

We've all known persons who triumph through illness and affliction — persons who bravely set the example for others. Fanny Crosby was such a person:

The famous blind songwriter Fanny Crosby wrote more than 8,000 songs. This fact and other interesting highlights in the life of Miss Crosby were revealed by Warren Wiersbe in his book Victorious Christian. Wiersbe explained that when Fanny was only 6 weeks old a minor eye inflammation developed. The doctor who treated the case was careless, though, and she became totally and permanently blind.

Fanny Crosby harbored no bitterness against the physician, however. In fact, she once said of him, "If I could meet him now, I would say thank you, over and over again for making me blind." She felt that her blindness was a gift from God to help her write the hymns that flowed from her pen. According to those who knew her, Miss Crosby probably would have refused treatment even if it could have assured the restoration of her sight.

Wiersbe concluded by commenting: "It was said of another blind hymnwriter, George Matheson, that God made him blind so he could see clearly in other ways and become a guide to men. This same tribute could be applied to Fanny Crosby, who triumphed over her handicap and used it to the glory of God." Yes, this talented woman allowed her tragedy to make her better instead of bitter.[2]

Suggested inclusions for letters, notes, and conversations:

Scriptures

James 5:16

> Therefore confess your sins to each other and pray for each other so that you may be healed. The prayer of a righteous man is powerful and effective.

Matthew 18:19

> "Again, I tell you that if two of you on earth agree about anything you ask for, it will be done for you by my Father in heaven."

Mark 11:24

> Therefore I tell you, whatever you ask for in prayer, believe that you have received it, and it will be yours.

I John 5:14-15

> 14 This is the confidence we have in approaching God: that if we ask anything according to his will, he hears us.
> 15 And if we know that he hears us—whatever we ask—we know that we have what we asked of him.

Romans 8: 28

And we know that in all things God works for the good of those who love him, who have been called according to his purpose.

Psalms 103:2-3

2 Praise the LORD, O my soul, and forget not all his benefits—

3 who forgives all your sins and heals all your diseases,

II Corinthians 4:17

For our light and momentary troubles are achieving for us an eternal glory that far outweighs them all.

Words to say

- We can become strong in our weakness.

- Counting our blessings helps us to forget how we feel.

- Reflect on times of good health.

- Think positive thoughts.

- One day we'll all have new, ache-free bodies.

- God is not punishing us when we're ill; He's perfecting us.

- God hears and answers our prayers in His way, His time.

- God loves you, in whatever physical condition

you find yourself.

- God doesn't always choose to heal us, but His plan is always best.

Words to pray — if you want to close your letter or conversation with a prayer, you might include:

- Praise to God for His healing power.

- Thanks to God for hearing prayers for wholeness.

- Prayer for insight as to what might be the cause of the illness.

- Prayer that God will provide rest for the one who is ill.

- Prayer for right relationships in the person's life.

- Prayer for Christian fellowship for the person.

Opportunity For Encouragement:

Grief Over Death of a Loved One

Throughout ages, humankind has grieved over the loss of loved ones. The hurt can cause us to feel alone even in a crowded room, because a special someone is no longer there. We can be aware of the steps we follow during the grieving process, yet we may not want to admit we are going through them. For Christians, the hope we share in Jesus Christ carries us through the deep pain we experience.

When my mother was killed in an automobile accident, I felt unsure of her salvation, although we had spoken often of our faith and I believed hers was strong. Having prayed during the long drive home that God would give me assurance that she was with Him, I should not have been surprised to feel the warmth of a soft blanket of peace and love fall over me as I walked into the funeral home. It was all I needed.

Everything was different with my father. Having spent long conversations with him, sharing the gospel and steps to salvation, there was no assurance. Shortly before his death, his words to me evidenced his belief in his own good works instead of Jesus Christ. Holding firm to my faith, I believed that God would meet him in his closing hours. I'll not know until I get to heaven if my prayers were answered.

If I see my earthly father again, I'll rejoice with the angels! If I don't, I have to believe that I won't miss him. I'd be sorrowful to know my father wasn't there, and we're told there will be no tears or sorrow in heaven. How God works this whole thing out, I don't know. I don't have to know. My peace comes knowing I shared all I could with my father. Our job is to share our faith. Salvation is God's business.

This story may help us put everything in the proper perspective:

Rev. Carl Burnham, beloved pastor of the Chapel on Fir Hill in Akron, Ohio, wrote in 1962, just prior to his Home-going, "When I die, if my family wishes to inscribe anything on my gravestone, I would like it to be the promise of Jesus Christ in Hebrews 13:5, 'I will never leave thee, nor forsake thee.' For in due season the springtime will arrive—then, when the resurrection sings itself in the robin's glad song, and bursting buds defy the death grip of winter, and you walk upon the yielding earth near my grave—remember that my soul is not there, but rather it is absent from the body, present with the Lord. And somewhere, the atoms that made up my brain, my heart—my body—will be sending out resurrection radiations of a frequency too high for any earthly Geiger counter to record. But if you place the meter of God's Word alongside that cemetery plot and adjust the settings to Hebrews 13:5, you will receive this reading: 'He hath said, I will never leave thee, nor forsake thee.'" [2]

Perhaps the best thing we can do to ease a friend's pain is to encourage them to talk about their loved one, special times together, special qualities. Memories are a precious gift to which we can cling. Sometimes words don't come easily when we visit with one in deep grief. Words don't have to be present if you are.

Suggested inclusions for letters, notes, and conversations:

Scriptures

Hebrews 13:5b

"...Never will I leave you; never will I forsake you."

John 14:1-3

1 "Do not let your hearts be troubled. Trust in God; trust also in me.

2 In my Father's house are many rooms; if it were not so, I would have told you. I am going there to prepare a place for you.

3 And if I go and prepare a place for you, I will come back and take you to be with me that you also may be where I am.

John 11:25

Jesus said to her, "I am the resurrection and the life. He who believes in me will live, even though he dies;

Philippians 1:21

For to me, to live is Christ and to die is gain

I Corinthians 2:9

However, as it is written: "No eye has seen, no ear has heard, no mind has conceived what God has prepared for those who love him—"

Revelation 21:4

"He will wipe every tear from their eyes. There will be no more death or mourning or crying or pain, for the old order of things has passed away."

Words to say

- There is so little I can say. But I'm here for you and I'll help in any way I can.
- Heaven is a better place since your loved one has arrived.
- I can almost hear the angels rejoicing.
- Tell me what you're thinking.
- Share with me a favorite story of your life together.
- Let me share what (the loved one) meant to me.
- Your (loved one) was a very special person. I'll always remember the time...
- It's wonderful to know you'll see each other again.
- Experiencing the death of a loved one can enrich our earthly relationship with Christ.
- When you're feeling lonely, remember God is with you.

Words to pray — if you want to close your letter or conversation with a prayer, you might include:

- Prayer that God will wrap His loving arms around the person.
- Prayer that God will give the person peace.

- Prayer that God will provide companionship in lonely hours.

- Prayer that God will bring many precious memories to mind.

Opportunity For Encouragement:

Financial Concerns

I've often wondered what it must be like to grow up in a wealthy family and perhaps never experience financial concerns. Maybe *everyone,* no matter how wealthy, faces financial concerns at one time or another.

My growing up years, as part of a large family on a small farm income, were stressful, to say the least. As number five of seven children, money for college education was scarce by the time my turn rolled around. It was like reaching into a barrel, and finding only the cold, bare bottom. Having struggled through college years, on a skimpy allowance budgeted to myself, I remember the fantastic joy of being hired for a teaching position upon graduation. A real paycheck!

Much later in my life, I came to know Jesus Christ. How exciting it was to become a member of God's family, belonging to the One who owns it all. Being a king's kid is awesome. Think about it. Our Father owns the cattle on a thousand hills, and, indeed, *everything* is His. We are but stewards; each of our possessions is a loan from Him. He has promised to meet our every need if we are living according to His righteousness. Our spiritual treasures are the only ones that count toward eternity.

Financial disagreement, or mishandling finances, is

recognized as a major cause of divorce. Understanding basic finances should be a high priority for everyone. Credit purchases, self-indulgent living, not following a budget, covetousness — all can contribute to financial concerns.

As parents, we should begin to teach our children at an early age how to be good stewards of money and possessions. We can't start too early to grow their understanding that all we have belongs to God. They will grow up with a confidence and security that some of us had to develop much later in life.

Allow these few words to sink into your heart:

The real measure of our wealth is how much we'd be worth if we lost all our money. - J.H. Jowett [2]

We must remember that money or wealth, in itself, is not bad. It's the love of that money, when we think more of it than we do of our Lord, when we serve money, rather than Jesus Christ, that is wrong. Scripture also teaches us to give cheerfully. Giving to God and His kingdom is the greatest kind of giving.

If a man's religion does not affect his use of money, that man's religion is vain. - Hugh Martin [2]

Suggested inclusions for letters, notes, and conversations:

Scriptures

Matthew 6:33

> But seek first his kingdom and his righteousness, and all these things will be given to you as well.

Philippians 4:19

> And my God will meet all your needs according to his glorious riches in Christ Jesus.

Luke 6:38

"Give, and it will be given to you. A good measure, pressed down, shaken together and running over, will be poured into your lap. For with the measure you use, it will be measured to you."

Ecclesiastes 5:10

Whoever loves money never has money enough; whoever loves wealth is never satisfied with his income. This too is meaningless.

Hebrews 13:5

Keep your lives free from the love of money and be content with what you have, because God has said, "Never will I leave you; never will I forsake you."

Matthew 6:19-21

19 "Do not store up for yourselves treasures on earth, where moth and rust destroy, and where thieves break in and steal.
20 But store up for yourselves treasures in heaven, where moth and rust do not destroy, and where thieves do not break in and steal.
21 For where your treasure is, there your heart will be also.

I Timothy 6:6-7

6 But godliness with contentment is great gain.
7 For we brought nothing into the world, and we can take nothing out of it.

Words to say

- If God is first in our lives, we can't go wrong.

- Our lives are far more important than our money.
- What is the worst thing that can happen if you run out of money?
- We can never outgive God.
- It's great to be a child of the King.
- Live one day at a time.
- Every possession we have belongs to God.
- God holds us accountable for His gifts to us.

Words to pray — if you want to close your letter or conversation with a prayer, you might include:

- Praise to God for His faithfulness.
- Praise to God for past blessings.
- Prayer that God would reveal His plan for the person's life; perhaps God has another vocation in mind.
- Prayer that the person will not grow weary, but remain strong.
- Prayer that the person's priorities will be put in the proper order.

Opportunity For Encouragement: Parent/Child Relationships

Each of us faced parent/child relationship problems as children growing up; we may be facing them now as a parent; we may be facing them now as a child *taking care of a parent.* We will always be in one role or another. Right relationships can be difficult to achieve and/or maintain. Yet, God desires families to live in harmony with each other and Him.

Conflict, lack of discipline, and rebellion frequently cause relational difficulties. Physical conditions of either the parent or child can enter in as well. If the family is centered around faith in Jesus Christ, the problems can be dealt with through prayer and much love; however, often one or more family members are not believers, causing a sensitive situation.

There is no guaranteed process for successfully raising children. A book proclaiming such a guarantee would surely be a best-seller. Watching children of many families grow and mature has been fascinating to me. My perspective has been gained from a distance — from the outside looking in, most of the time.

I've watched as children raised in homes of successful, financially secure parents have gone off to college, received graduate degrees and entered into equal or greater success than their parents. Rolling along the tracks of motivation and discipline, these children have been guided like smoothly running trains. Others in similar situations have dropped out of high school or college, totally lacking direction and motivation, as if derailed from the tracks placed directly in front of them.

I've seen children raised in the home of heavy drinkers disavow any drinking activity in their own lives. Others have taken a different attitude: "What's OK for Mom and Dad is OK for me."

I've seen children from impoverished homes conquer all odds to become great leaders. Determination, like dynamite placed into heavy rock, has blasted them through. Others, sadly defeated as children, have themselves become the blasted particles.

Love seems to be the ingredient that never fails in our pursuit to raise healthy, successful children. Sometimes it must be tough love, but love will prevail. Many parents who have continued to love their children through rebellion and conflict have gratefully watched their prodigals return at some point in life.

Let me share this story of a prodigal:

A man was successful in business, and had a well-educated son who was highly respected and honored like his father. But one day to everyone's surprise the young man was charged with embezzlement. At his trial he appeared nonchalant and arrogant about his sinful actions. When the judge told him to stand up for sentencing, he still seemed unrepentant. Then hearing a slight scuffle on the other side of the room, he turned to see that his aged father had also risen. The once erect head and straight shoulders of that honest man were now bowed low with shame. He had stood to be identified with his boy and to receive the verdict as though it were being pronounced upon himself. Suddenly his son realized the terrible grief he was inflicting on him, and tears welled up in his eyes. He had tarnished the family name by his behavior. Now his poor father was caught in the backwash of his son's evil deeds, although he had done everything he could do to keep him on the straight and narrow path. [2]

Suggested inclusions for letters, notes, and conversations:

Scriptures

Deuteronomy 6:6-9

6 These commandments that I give you today are to be upon your hearts.
7 Impress them on your children. Talk about them when you sit at home and when you walk along the road, when you lie down and when you get up.
8 Tie them as symbols on your hands and bind them on your foreheads.
9 Write them on the doorframes of your houses and on your gates.

Deuteronomy 12:28

Be careful to obey all these regulations I am giving you, so that it may always go well with you and your children after you, because you will be doing what is good and right in the eyes of the LORD your God.

Proverbs 20:7

The righteous man leads a blameless life; blessed are his children after him.

Ephesians 6:1-3

1 Children, obey your parents in the Lord, for this is right.
2 "Honor your father and mother"—which is the first commandment with a promise—
3 "that it may go well with you and that you may

enjoy long life on the earth."

Colossians 3:20

Fathers, do not embitter your children, or they will become discouraged.

Words to say

- Love is the one lasting gift that we can give our children.
- If we listen with our hearts, we can learn from our children.
- We need to love our children, even when we don't like what they do.
- Parents have to be as flexible as bendable straws.
- Be open and honest.
- It's important that we keep our promises.
- Just be there for your children.
- Sometimes it's hard to *like* our children; *love* comes more easily.
- Trust and honesty are key ingredients to successful parenting.
- Practice love in action, not just in words.
- Be generous with forgiveness.

- Discipline with love and consistency.

- "I love you," said often and sincerely, are the best words of all.

- Give hugs as often as possible.

- Practice respect for one another.

Words to pray — if you want to close your letter or conversation with a prayer, you might include:

- Prayer that God will have His rightful place in the person's home.

- Prayer that God will fill the parent's heart with deep, sincere love for every child, even one that errs.

- Prayer that the parents will set a solid example of Christian love.

- Prayer that broken relationships will be restored.

- Prayer that the parents will find forgiveness for past conflicts, hurts.

- Prayer that there will be peace in the hearts of family members.

Opportunity For Encouragement:

Depression/Discouragement

Depression/discouragement is one of the most common emotional problems any of us experience. I personally describe it as those times when I "just can't get on top of things," or "don't feel like doing anything." It's like having a weight upon my shoulders, holding me down, causing me to drag along slowly. Depression is very normal. I've never known anyone to escape it completely, though surely some persons are more victorious over it than others.

Depression, in general, is difficult to define. For me, it's usually short-lived; for many, it lasts a long time and can become a serious illness. A few of the symptoms are hopelessness, inadequacy, gloominess, inability to think straight, lack of energy, sadness, and poor self-image, to name just a few.

Depressed persons may blame others for their emotional state, dumping garbage on them. Although garbage dumping may help momentarily, it won't be a permanent fix. Our feelings are our own. Spontaneous, they can't be dictated or planned. Blaming others doesn't help us to honestly deal with them.

We are personally responsible for both our feelings and what we do with them. Feelings, in themselves, can't be labeled right or wrong. They're as neutral as the proverbial fence we often sit on. However, if we allow negative feelings to lead us to hurt others, we sin.

If we sense a person is depressed or discouraged, we should avoid pointing sharp fingers of accusation at them. We've probably had the same feeling at one time or another. Telling them it's wrong to feel the way they do, or to snap out of it sounds easy to us, but impossible to them. Their feeling is real. Instead, we should give assurance that it's all right to feel like they do. Gently asking questions may help the person to understand the cause of the feeling.

If you suspect someone is depressed, be a good listener, compassionate and understanding. Be an encourager. And maintain *confidentiality*. Serious damage can occur if something said in confidence gets back to the depressed person. It's important to build up trust, not tear it down.

Determining the cause of depression is critical, and this can be a long process in serious cases of depression. Seriously depressed persons should seek professional counsel, and often that, in itself, takes encouragement. A letter or note of encouragement can very positively impact a person suffering from depression or discouragement.

Charles Spurgeon, called to a church at 23, addressing crowds of 5,000 at 30, wrote this:

Before any great achievement in my life, some measure of depression is very usual. Such was my experience when I first became a pastor in London; my success appalled me and the thought of that career which seemed to be opening up, so far from elating me, cast me into the lowest depths out of which I uttered my misery. I found no room for a Gloria in Excelsis.

Who was I that I should continue to lead so great a multitude? I would slip away to my village obscurity or prefer to emigrate to America and find a solitary nest in the backwoods.

It was just then that the curtain was rising on my greatest life's work and I dreaded what it might reveal to me. I hope I was not faithless! But I was timorous and filled with a sense of my own unfitness. This depression sweeps over me whenever the Lord is preparing a larger blessing for my life and ministry.

Some of you are right at the door. [2]

Suggested inclusions for letters, notes, and conversations:

Scriptures

Romans 8:28

And we know that in all things God works for the good of those who love him, who have been called according to his purpose.

I Thessalonians 5:18

Give thanks in all circumstances, for this is God's will for you in Christ Jesus.

Matthew 11: 28-30

28 "Come to me, all you who are weary and burdened, and I will give you rest.
29 Take my yoke upon you and learn from me, for I am gentle and humble in heart, and you will find rest for your souls.
30 For my yoke is easy and my burden is light."

Philippians 4:13

I can do everything through him who gives me strength.

II Timothy 1:7

For God did not give us a spirit of timidity, but a spirit of power, of love and of self-discipline.

I Corinthians 15:10

But by the grace of God I am what I am, and his grace to me was not without effect. No, I worked harder than all of them—yet not I, but the grace of God that was with me.

II Corinthians 4:8-9

8 We are hard pressed on every side, but not crushed; perplexed, but not in despair;
9 persecuted, but not abandoned; struck down, but not destroyed.

Galations 2:20

I have been crucified with Christ and I no longer live, but Christ lives in me. The life I live in the body, I live by faith in the Son of God, who loved me and gave himself for me.

Psalm 34:17

The righteous cry out, and the LORD hears them; he delivers them from all their troubles.

John 14:1

"Do not let your hearts be troubled. Trust in God; trust also in me."

Words to say

- If you want to share with me what is bothering you, I'll be happy to listen.

- You can trust me to hold what you say in confidence.
- Perhaps you are expecting too much of yourself.
- I am here for you, to give you whatever support I can give.
- You have so often been there for me—now let me help you.
- God cares. He will not leave you alone.
- Going through this difficult time can help you to become strong and special. I believe you will see your way through this.
- Just remember, you are not alone — many of us are thinking of you and praying for you.
- God is holding you in the palm of His hands. His arms are wrapped around you.
- God is pleased when you lean on Him.
- God has given you unique abilities, strengths and limitations. Try to learn to accept them.
- Spend time in God's word.

Words to pray—if you want to close your letter or conversation with a prayer, you might include:

- Thanks for God and His love.
- Belief that God can uplift our spirits.

- Praise to Jesus for bearing not only our sins, but our sorrows and heartaches.

- Praise that God never leaves us alone.

- Prayer that the person will be able to trust God fully in all areas of life.

Opportunity For Encouragement:

Fear of Death

Believers in Jesus Christ have the blessed assurance of eternal life in His presence. I Corinthians 15:54 tells us that "death has been swallowed up in victory." Physical death is but a transition from earthly to heavenly life; our spirits immediately go into the Lord's presence, enriching our relationship with Him. Luke 23:43 makes it clear: Jesus, turning to the repentant thief on the cross next to Him, said, "I tell you the truth, today you will be with me in paradise."

As believers, we know that our earthly bodies will one day become new, permanent, and, indeed, glorious. Whether we are alive when Christ returns or have already turned to dust, a new spiritual body awaits us. This is a wondrous thought as aches, pains, and age spots, a sagging chin, and bulging hips remind me that I'm not what I used to be.

On one hand, my competitive nature causes me to hope that I die before Christ returns, so that I am among the first to receive my new heavenly body. This desire is based on I Thessalonians 4:16, stating that "the dead in Christ will rise first." On the other hand, I've always wondered what it would be like to fly like an angel. It would be neat to be alive and to be "caught up in the air" with the Lord.

We can encourage believers, as Paul did in Philippians 1:21, "For to me, to live is Christ and to die is gain." Now, please don't get me wrong — living is very important. Watching my grandchildren grow up, serving the Lord I love, and enjoying a productive, healthy retirement are foremost in my mind. Yet, my confidence in Christ's promises keeps me at peace.

My deepest concern over death is for those I will leave behind, assuming, of course, that my life has impacted them positively in some way. My assurance to any believer left behind is that I *will* see them again. Perhaps that is why I try to never say good-bye to a brother or sister in Christ. For believers in the fellowship of Christ, there will be no good-bye — only farewell, until we meet at the foot of Jesus.

This short excerpt confirms that thought:

Phillips Brooks of Boston became quite ill and would see no visitors. When Robert Ingersoll, the agnostic, heard that his friend was sick, he called at his home and was admitted at once. "I appreciate this very much," said Mr. Ingersoll. "But why do you see me when you deny yourself to your other friends."

"It is this way," answered Bishop Brooks. "I feel confident of seeing my other friends in the next world, but this may be my last chance to see you." - Emery Young, in Coronet from *The Sermon Builder*, February 1982, p. 34.[2]

Suggested inclusions for letters, notes, and conversations:

Scriptures

John 11:25-26

> 25 Jesus said to her, "I am the resurrection and the life. He who believes in me will live, even though he dies;
> 26 and whoever lives and believes in me will never

die. Do you believe this?"

Psalms 23:4

Even though I walk through the valley of the shadow of death, I will fear no evil, for you are with me; your rod and your staff, they comfort me.

Matthew 10:39

Whoever finds his life will lose it, and whoever loses his life for my sake will find it.

Revelation 22:5

There will be no more night. They will not need the light of a lamp or the light of the sun, for the Lord God will give them light. And they will reign for ever and ever.

John 3:16

"For God so loved the world that he gave his one and only Son, that whoever believes in him shall not perish but have eternal life."

Philippians 1:21

For to me, to live is Christ and to die is gain.

John 14:1-3

1 "Do not let your hearts be troubled. Trust in God; trust also in me.
2 In my Father's house are many rooms; if it were not so, I would have told you. I am going there to prepare a place for you.
3 And if I go and prepare a place for you, I will come back and take you to be with me that you also may be where I am.

Words to say

- Imagine sitting at the feet of Jesus!
- What's the first thing you'll ask Jesus when you see Him?
- Following Christ as an earthly believer can't come close to the thought of being with Him, watching and listening firsthand.
- Jesus left the earth to prepare a place for you. Think about that.
- Can you imagine never being sad, lonely, discouraged or sick ever again?
- We can look forward to reunions with loved ones.
- How exciting it will be to have a heavenly new body!
- Life, for a believer, is a never ending circle.
- Death is merely our transportation vehicle to heaven.

Words to pray — if you want to close your letter or conversation with a prayer, you might include:

- Prayer for perfect peace, that death is not to be feared.
- Praise that God sent his Son, to show us the way to eternal life with Him.

- Prayer that the person can overcome fearful thoughts with good, lovely, true, right thoughts.

- Prayer for confidence that the person will be with God forever.

Opportunity For Encouragement:

Guilt

Guilt and guilt feelings are the cause of many other problems and concerns in life. Real guilt occurs anytime we do, think or say something that is wrong and against God's commandments. It comes as a result of sin from breaking God's law. The Holy Spirit of God speaks to our spirits, convicting us of our wrongdoing. When we sin, our relationship with God is broken. As Christians, we have the privilege of confessing our sin, being freed from guilt, and having our relationship restored.

Guilt *feelings*, on the other hand, may stem from negative childhood experiences. Guilt feelings that linger can lead to emotional illness. They may have nothing to do with breaking God's law. Persons with these feelings often cannot get rid of them, despite sincere efforts to do so. They feel inadequate or depressed. They might develop defeatist attitudes that will cause them to sink deeper into guilt feelings.

I wonder how many other persons are like myself. I can *feel* guilty over very little, insignificant things — an oversight in my daily routine, being thoughtless in some situation, or knowing I didn't give my best in some activity. When I feel guilty, I'm not myself. I might act angry or be uptight. I might eat too much, or not enough. (For me, it's usually too much!) I probably don't sleep well, resulting in a short temper, impatience, and perhaps even depression.

Real guilt, brought on by sin, is often easier to deal with. Thank God, we can confess our sin to get rid of this guilt, and be assured that God has forgiven it. Sometimes, however, we hang on to guilt for a while, refusing to admit we were wrong. Confession to God is the easy part — after all, we are only agreeing with what He already knows; confession to the one I may have offended is much harder. Confession includes seeking forgiveness.

You might find the following as interesting as I did:

A new product called "Disposable Guilt Bags" appeared in the marketplace. It consisted of a set of ten ordinary brown bags on which were printed the following instructions: "Place the bag securely over your mouth, take a deep breath and blow all your guilt out, then dispose of the bag immediately." The wonder of this is that the Associated Press reported that 2,500 kits had been quickly sold at $2.50 per kit. Would that we could dispose of our guilt so easily. There is nothing on this earth powerful enough in itself to dispose of our guilt. We cannot fix ourselves, which is what many of us are trying to do. That which makes it possible to be forgiven, to be cleansed, to be healed, that which makes it possible for us to receive our life back again, fresh and clean and new, is the power of God's Grace in the Cross of Jesus Christ. [2]

Suggested inclusions for letters, notes, and conversations:

Scriptures

Isaiah 44:22

> "I have swept away your offenses like a cloud, your sins like the morning mist. Return to me, for I

have redeemed you."

Isaiah 1:18

"Come now, let us reason together," says the LORD. "Though your sins are like scarlet, they shall be as white as snow; though they are red as crimson, they shall be like wool."

Matthew 6:14

For if you forgive men when they sin against you, your heavenly Father will also forgive you.

Romans 6:23

For the wages of sin is death, but the gift of God is eternal life in Christ Jesus our Lord.

I John 1:9

If we confess our sins, he is faithful and just and will forgive us our sins and purify us from all unrighteousness.

Romans 8:1-2

1 Therefore, there is now no condemnation for those who are in Christ Jesus,
2 because through Christ Jesus the law of the Spirit of life set me free from the law of sin and death.

John 8:36

So if the Son sets you free, you will be free indeed.

Philippians 3: 13-14

13 Brothers, I do not consider myself yet to have taken hold of it. But one thing I do: Forgetting what is behind and straining toward what is ahead,
14 I press on toward the goal to win the prize for

which God has called me heavenward in Christ Jesus.

Words to say

- We know we're forgiven, because God said He'd forgive us.

- Pretend you've written your sin on a blackboard. God holds the eraser.

- Sometimes it's hard to be honest with God, but confessing sin is just agreeing with what He already knows.

- We'll never be perfect, but we are forgiven.

- Guilt from sin is like a boulder in the middle of the road that diverts our path; it keeps us from being where we'd like to be.

- After we ask for forgiveness, we need to believe that we have received it.

- Learn to forgive yourself.

- We grow from our mistakes.

Words to pray — if you want to close your letter or conversation with a prayer, you might include:

- Prayer that the person will have assurance of God's forgiveness.

- Prayer that the person can forgive themselves.

- Prayer that the person will be able to seek forgiveness from those who have been offended.
- Thanking God that there is no condemnation for those of us in Christ Jesus.
- Prayer that the joy of the Lord will return.

Opportunity For Encouragement:

Bitterness and Resentment

My understanding of bitterness and resentment has grown as I've watched it impact persons I love. The initial cause of bitterness is usually anger, when one individual is offended, disappointed, or mistreated by another individual. The angry feeling, like a seed, is allowed to germinate and grow, rather than being resolved immediately. Cultivated this way, the anger blooms like an undesirable flower, resulting in bitterness, often destroying relationships. Unforgiving spirits and critical attitudes may result.

Eventually, mental, physical, or spiritual health may be seriously affected by bottled up feelings. Like depression and stress, unresolved bitterness is sinful. It is necessary to seek forgiveness from God and from the person against whom the grudge is held. Jesus can remove the rage that we feel within our hearts.

We know that God both forgives and *forgets* our past sin when we confess it. Taking His sharpest shears, He cuts away that section of the film of our life and destroys it.

It's not easy for us to *forget* past hurts, as hard as we try, even when we are willing to forgive. God can help our way of remembering, however — He can help us to remember with forgiveness rather than hostility and hurt.

I share this story about bitterness:

Recently I read about a woman who, on the advice of her doctor, had gone to see a pastor to talk about joining the church. She had recently had a facelift and when her doctor dismissed her, he gave her this advice:

"My dear, I have done an extraordinary job on your face, as you can see in the mirror. I have charged you a great deal of money and you were happy to pay it. But I want to give you some free advice. Find a group of people who love God and who will love you enough to help you deal with all the negative emotions inside of you. If you don't you'll be back in my office in a very short time with your face in far worse shape than before." —*There's a Lot More to Health Than Not Being Sick,* Bruce Larson [2]

Suggested inclusions for letters, notes, and conversations:

Scriptures

Psalms 37:8

Refrain from anger and turn from wrath; do not fret—it leads only to evil.

Proverbs 15:1

A gentle answer turns away wrath, but a harsh word stirs up anger.

Proverbs 19:11

A man's wisdom gives him patience; it is to his glory to overlook an offense.

Proverbs 29:11

A fool gives full vent to his anger, but a wise man keeps himself under control.

James 1:19-20

19 My dear brothers, take note of this: Everyone
should be quick to listen, slow to speak and slow to
become angry,
20 for man's anger does not bring about the righteous life that God desires.

Hebrews 12:14-15

14 Make every effort to live in peace with all men
and to be holy; without holiness no one will see the
Lord.
15 See to it that no one misses the grace of God and
that no bitter root grows up to cause trouble and
defile many.

Matthew 6:14-15

14 For if you forgive men when they sin against
you, your heavenly Father will also forgive you.
15 But if you do not forgive men their sins, your
Father will not forgive your sins.

Colossians 3:8

But now you must rid yourselves of all such things as these: anger, rage, malice, slander, and filthy language from your lips.

Romans 14:13

Therefore let us stop passing judgment on one another. Instead, make up your mind not to put any stumbling block or obstacle in your brother's way.

Words to say

- Everyone becomes bitter at times; it's part of our

sinful nature.

- Anger, in itself, is not sinful; it's when we let it remain and grow that it becomes sinful.

- God loves us, even when we feel resentment, but He wants us to give it up.

- God knows how you feel, but tell Him anyway. He's waiting to hear from you.

- When we allow resentment to breed, it's like a noose around our necks.

- Bitterness builds nasty walls between persons.

Words to pray — if you want to close your letter or conversation with a prayer, you might include:

- Asking God to help the person forgive the offender and forget the hurt within him/her.

- Asking God to forgive the person for allowing bitterness to grow.

- Prayer that God will cleanse the person's memory.

- Prayer that the person can confess his/her feelings to God.

Opportunity For Encouragement:

Lack of Faith

Faith is a gift of God. According to Ephesians 2:8, "For it is by grace you have been saved, through faith—and this not from yourselves, it is the gift of God..."

Faith, the greatest of God's gifts, is also the most necessary. When we find ourselves unable to trust God and His Word, we lack this greatest gift of all. Lacking faith, we sin.

Faith in Jesus Christ is the absolute requirement for eternal life. When we become believers in Jesus Christ, experiencing new life in Him, we are given faith — saving faith. Our new life in Christ begins a *forever* relationship for the remainder of our earthly life and into eternity. Yet, we often find ourselves falling short in the faith department, simply because we don't exercise faith daily — mountain moving faith.

God's word assures us that He will meet our needs... that He is merciful and loving...that He is holy and faithful. God's faith is big enough to sustain all of us in all circumstances. But, in addition to believing, we must "live by faith." When a lack of faith overcomes us, we need only to ask God to help us through, to conquer our uncertainty. Lack of faith is a negative condition not worthy of our God, with Whom nothing is impossible.

Faith can so easily slip through our fingers when we are going through difficult, discouraging times. We find ourselves groping for faith, struggling to grasp it, like an elusive soap bubble. And just when we think we have it, it might pop and we have to start all over again. Occasionally, giving up seems to be our easiest choice, and we succumb to the temptation. When it comes to faith, we should listen to what Jesus tells us and not to the voices of others. Jesus said, "Have faith in God." (Mark 11:22)

Let me illustrate examples of mountain moving faith through the following:

I've been thinking recently about how glad I am that certain visionaries refused to listen to the frowning crowd on the pier. I'm glad, for example:

* *that Edison didn't give up on the light bulb even though his helpers seriously doubted the thing would ever work.*
* *that Luther refused to back down when the church doubled her fists and clenched her teeth.*
* *that Michaelangelo kept pounding and painting, regardless of those negative put-downs.*
* *that Lindbergh decided to ignore what everyone else had said was ridiculous and flirting with death.*
* *that Douglas MacArthur promised, during the darkest days of World War II, "I shall return."*
* *that Papa Ten Boom said "Yes" to frightened Jews who needed a safe refuge, a hiding place.*
* *that the distinguished Julliard School of Music would see beyond the braces and wheelchair and admit an unlikely violin student named Perlman.*
* *that Tom Sullivan decided to be everything that he could possibly be even though he was born blind.*
* *that the Gaithers made room in their busy lives for a scared young soprano who would one day thrill Christendom with "We Shall Behold Him."*

** that Fred Dixon continued to train for the decathlon — and finished the course — even though critics told him he was over the hill.*
** that our Lord Jesus held nothing back when He left heaven, lived on earth, and went for it — all the way to the cross — and beyond.*

You could add to the list. You may even belong on the list. If so, hats off to you. [2]

Suggested inclusions for letters, notes, and conversations:

Scriptures

Hebrews 12:1-3

> 1 Therefore, since we are surrounded by such a great cloud of witnesses, let us throw off everything that hinders and the sin that so easily entangles, and let us run with perseverance the race marked out for us.
> 2 Let us fix our eyes on Jesus, the author and perfecter of our faith, who for the joy set before him endured the cross, scorning its shame, and sat down at the right hand of the throne of God.
> 3 Consider him who endured such opposition from sinful men, so that you will not grow weary and lose heart.

Romans 10:17

> Consequently, faith comes from hearing the message, and the message is heard through the word of Christ.

Matthew 17:20

> He replied, "Because you have so little faith. I tell you the truth, if you have faith as small as a mustard

seed, you can say to this mountain, 'Move from here to there' and it will move. Nothing will be impossible for you."

John 3:16

"For God so loved the world that he gave his one and only Son, that whoever believes in him shall not perish but have eternal life."

Romans 5:1

Therefore, since we have been justified through faith, we have peace with God through our Lord Jesus Christ.

Mark 11: 22

"Have faith in God," Jesus answered.

Words to say

- Our faith is like our automobile—sometimes it needs a tuneup.
- Ask others to share what God has done for them.
- With God, all things are possible.
- Think positive thoughts.
- Think back on your life and all God has done for you.
- True faith results in action. Help yourself by helping others.
- Exercise faith in your prayer life — pray believing

God for His best answers.

- Exercise spiritual discipline to develop strong faith — read, study God's word.

- Look around you — at small plants that struggle to grow through cracks, at tiny insects carrying big objects, at intricate flowers— and marvel at God's creation.

Words to pray — if you want to close your letter or conversation with a prayer, you might include:

- Prayer that the person can confess his/her lack of faith; ask God to build it up.

- Telling God that you believe He will give this person the faith he/she needs.

- Praise Him for all that He has done for this person.

- Prayer that God will bring to the person's mind all that He has done for him/her.

Opportunity For Encouragement:

Loneliness

When I feel lonely, I may feel worthless. Tears fall easily. I may feel sorry for myself, rejected, unwanted, like the ugly duckling. Fortunately, my loneliness usually comes and goes quickly. That's not the case for many others, who truly are lonely throughout much of life. The important thing for those of us experiencing loneliness is the realization that we are truly never alone. God has promised us that He is always with us.

In this age of mobility, as families are moved at the drop of a hat, loneliness impacts each member of the family. How good it is to know that God moves with us. He's there when we're uprooted and moved across country, when we're subjected to constant change. He inhabits our new homes before we do, and knew long before we did that we'd be in each place we call home. He's the first one there to greet us. Neighbors often take longer.

He's with us when meaningful relationships appear to be as far away as east is from west. He's with us when our lonely self-image is not one we want to see peering back from the mirror — when we don't even like being with ourselves.

Prisoners may experience more loneliness than any other persons, especially if they're non-Christians. Yet, they can be encouraged to commit their lives to Jesus Christ, who will sit with them through lonely hours. Ministering to the needs of saved and unsaved prisoners through letters or notes can be truly life-saving.

Letters to the lonely often take the place of having someone there. Letters and notes can fill a void in a long, empty day, offering cheer and a presence. Holding onto a letter connects a lonely person with a real, caring person — an encourager...a life saver.

Thomas Wolfe has said:

"The whole conviction of my life now rests upon the belief that loneliness, far from being a rare and curious phenomenon, peculiar to myself and a few other solitary men, is the central and inevitable fact of human existence." We are told that, after a visit to the palace to visit with Queen Victoria, the great poet Alfred Lord Tennyson commented, "Up there, in all her glory and splendor, she was lonely." Nothing, whether it is royal status, wealth, public success, or bustling activism, can remove that need we have for other people.[2]

Suggested inclusions for letters, notes, and conversations:

Scriptures

Isaiah 54:10

> "Though the mountains be shaken and the hills be removed, yet my unfailing love for you will not be shaken nor my covenant of peace be removed," says the LORD, who has compassion on you.

I Corinthians 1:9

> God, who has called you into fellowship with his Son Jesus Christ our Lord, is faithful.

Revelation 3:20

Here I am! I stand at the door and knock. If anyone hears my voice and opens the door, I will come in and eat with him, and he with me.

Hebrews 13:5b

...God has said, "Never will I leave you; never will I forsake you."

Matthew 28:20b

"...And surely I am with you always, to the very end of the age."

John 14:18

I will not leave you as orphans; I will come to you.

Words to say

- Jesus is a friend who will stick closer than a brother.
- God is our constant companion.
- Often, serving others is the best way to overcome loneliness. How can you help others?
- You are important to me. You are important to God.
- I think of you and pray for you often.
- I'm concerned about your loneliness. How can I help?
- Have you talked with your Pastor about this?

- Keeping family relationships strong is key to feeling we belong.

- When I feel lonely, I find daily quiet time with God helps diminish the loneliness.

- How about lunch some day next week?

Words to pray — if you want to close your letter or conversation with a prayer, you might include:

- Praise that God is always at our side.

- Prayer that the person might find someone who also needs a friend.

- Prayer that the person would expect God to meet their need for companionship.

- Prayer that the person might find Christian fellowship.

Opportunity For Encouragement:

Fear

Fear, in a moderate sense of the word, is normal and, at times, even healthy. Fear can be a reaction to both imagined and real situations. We've all felt our hearts pounding or our palms sweating as we prepare to do something out of the ordinary. A certain amount of fear can keep us from being overconfident or careless as we prepare for a task.

Fear can also warn us of danger. Some of us have experienced that inner sense of knowing we must be careful as we approach an icy bridge in cold, wet weather, or cautious as we step on a wet, slippery rock at the edge of a precipice.

Yet, some persons appear to be fearful about everything and seem to want to pass it on to others with constant fear inducing comments. Today's world can indeed be a frightening place in which to live. Murders, drugs, abuse of all kinds, and pornography are just some of the things that run rampant. We are told and believe that God is in control. Despite that knowledge, doubt often silently creeps in like spiders into an open crack. We wonder if God knows what He is doing, and why He doesn't just stop the misdoings of our evil world.

As believers in Jesus Christ, we have nothing to fear.

Our righteousness in Him ensures eternity with Him, no matter what happens today, tomorrow, or further into the future. Fear, when we allow it to manipulate us, becomes a great enemy of faith. Fear is what we feel when faith is lacking. We can't experience both at once.

Fear often surprises us, happening at times we would not have suspected. Perhaps an unpleasant experience has convinced us that it could happen again. Allowing that thought to dwell in us, we become even more fearful.

When we find ourselves being fearful, it is helpful to dwell on God, praise Him, and repeat His words, "fear not," until faith overtakes the fear. This might take only a short while, or a considerable period of time.

Here are some insights regarding fear:

Probably the greatest book on fear ever written in this country was by Basil King and the title was The Conquest of Fear. *Here is the quotation: "Go at it boldly, and you'll find unexpected forces closing round you and coming to your aid." Isn't that terrific? "Go at it boldly, and you'll find unexpected forces closing round you and coming to your aid."*

Long before Basil King, Emerson said, "Do the thing you fear, and the death of fear is certain." You defeat worry and fear by filling your mind with the certain faith that you can do it. That is the best way to get rid of the worry and fear about those many things that are bothering you. Get out of yourself and do something about it, realizing that your Heavenly Father says to you, "For I, the Lord your God, hold your right hand; it is I who say to you, 'Fear not, I will help you.'" [2]

Suggested inclusions for letters, notes, and conversations:

Scriptures

John 10:14

"I am the good shepherd; I know my sheep and my sheep know me—

Matthew 10:29-31

29 Are not two sparrows sold for a penny? Yet not one of them will fall to the ground apart from the will of your Father.
30 And even the very hairs of your head are all numbered.
31 So don't be afraid; you are worth more than many sparrows.

Jeremiah 29:11

"For I know the plans I have for you," declares the LORD, "plans to prosper you and not to harm you, plans to give you hope and a future."

Psalms 27:1

The LORD is my light and my salvation—whom shall I fear? The LORD is the stronghold of my life—of whom shall I be afraid?

Isaiah 41:10

So do not fear, for I am with you; do not be dismayed, for I am your God. I will strengthen you and help you; I will uphold you with my righteous right hand.

II Timothy 1:7

For God did not give us a spirit of timidity, but a

spirit of power, of love and of self-discipline.

II Timothy 1:12b

...Yet I am not ashamed, because I know whom I have believed, and am convinced that he is able to guard what I have entrusted to him for that day.

Psalm 34:4

I sought the LORD, and he answered me; he delivered me from all my fears.

I John 4:18

There is no fear in love. But perfect love drives out fear, because fear has to do with punishment. The one who fears is not made perfect in love.

I John 4:4

You, dear children, are from God and have overcome them, because the one who is in you is greater than the one who is in the world.

Words to say

- Give each day to the Lord and ask Him to walk with you through it.
- Repeat one of the above scriptures over and over again.
- Our powerful, creator God has promised He is always with us.
- It helps to replace fearful thoughts with thoughts of love.

- We can do all things through Christ, who strengthens us.

- Delight in God and love Him completely. He'll drive out our fears.

- Expect the peace of God to fill you when it is most needed.

- Seek the companionship of strong Christian friends.

- Picture a guardian angel at the side of you and your loved ones.

- Remember that nothing can separate you from God's love.

- Let the giant God within you look fear in the face.

Words to pray — if you want to close your letter or conversation with a prayer, you might include:

- Asking God to surround the person with angels.

- Prayer for boldness to overcome the fear.

- Praise to God for His goodness and power in overcoming evil.

- Prayer for peace in fearful situations.

- Prayer that God will provide all the person's needs when needed.

Opportunity For Encouragement:

Being Falsely Accused

Their words pierced, hurting deeply. My husband and I had been falsely, unfairly accused by persons we love. Perhaps, had we been targeted privately with their unkind and untrue words, the hurt would have only stung like that of a mosquito bite. But, at the time, the manner in which the unfair words were spread caused the sting to be more like that of a viper.

False accusations are tough to live with — especially when they come from persons we love. It seemed the label slapped on the outside of us didn't match that which we believed was inside — honesty, uprightness, and commitment. It took a long time for me, especially, to grapple with and accept the fact that I did not have to believe what others said or thought. Standing before God in confidence that we had done what was right, answering to Him alone, was our greatest concern.

When we are falsely accused, we should not return lies with lies. Often, unkind retaliation is the first thought. We're all human. It's important to respond, however, and to respond honestly. God never intended for us to be trampled over like doormats. If we are willing to forgive, He knows it. If others refuse to acknowledge their offense against us, we can still love them. Love is not a feeling — it is a decision.

When we are falsely accused, we seem to think that *everyone* has poor impressions of us. Our sense of pride flairs up — our righteous indignation grows like corn in a hot, well-watered summer. Often, when a lie is told, it spreads like wildfire, and our imagination envisions it spreading worse than it actually does. Mark Twain said, "A lie can travel half way around the world while the truth is putting on its shoes."[2]

Most of us, at one time or another, have been victims of false accusations. God works for good in these situations, giving us an opportunity to grow and to encourage others in similar situations. We become more sensitive to what falsehoods, even little ones, can do. A person's reputation is important, and tearing it down can be devastating. When we slip, and we all do, confession erases our burden. If one of our slips is hurtful to another, we must confess and ask their forgiveness.

Those who are unfairly under attack need compassion. Most of what is said about us is minimal compared to that which others have suffered. Take, for example, those who have spent long years in prison only to be cleared later for crimes they did not commit. Others have lost jobs and leadership positions. Some have been stripped of parental privileges. False accusations leave an imprint like that of a foot stepping on newly poured concrete — they leave a lasting mark.

Scriptures have much to say about making false accusations. Deuteronomy 5:20 tells us "You shall not give false testimony against your neighbor." A "lying tongue" is among those things the Lord hates, according to Proverbs 6:17. God's stand on falsehood is clear, whether we are the inflictor or the inflictee. We can believe He stands with us when falsehoods are spoken against us, just as He wants us to ask forgiveness when we wrong others.

There is yet one more dimension to this area of false

accusation — being falsely accused because of our faith in Jesus Christ. All over the world, Christians are going through severe persecution because of their faith. Matthew 5: 11 addresses this: "Blessed are you when people insult you, persecute you and falsely say all kinds of evil against you because of me." Verse 12 follows with words of wisdom to use in this situation: "Rejoice and be glad, because great is your reward in heaven, for in the same way they persecuted the prophets who were before you."

Rejoicing is not the *natural or easy* response when we are treated unfairly because of our faith. It's helpful if we can remember to rejoice *in spite* of rather than *for* what we are going through. Letting others know of our own struggles with rejoicing makes us more real as we reach out to them. Our confidence comes in knowing the source of those words, and that God surely did not expect it to be easy.

Two thousand years ago, on a barren hillside, a young man, falsely accused, took my place and yours on a roughly hewn cross. He knows about false testimony and the pain it inflicts. In all situations, God already knows the truth. If we can confidently stand with Him in agreement, we should not be afraid. Yet, we must always be open to what He might have to say to us.

Here's some great advice about undue affliction:

We are told that pearls are the product of pain. When the shell of an oyster is chipped or pierced by a worm or boring parasite, a foreign substance, usually a grain of sand, gets in. The inside of an oyster's shell is made up of a lustrous substance called nacre. When a grain of sand gets into a shell, the nacre cells get busy. They cover the grain of sand with layer after layer of nacre in order to protect the soft body of the oyster. The result is that a beautiful pearl is formed. An oyster which has not been hurt does not grow a pearl—for a pearl is a healed wound.

Have you been hurt by an unkind word of a friend? Have you been accused of saying that which you have not said? Have you worked hard in the church and had no one express appreciation? Have your ideas been rebuffed? Then grow a pearl. Cover your hurts and your rebuffs with layer after layer of love. Just remember that an oyster which has not been hurt does not grow a pearl—for a pearl is a healed wound.—The Lamplighter [2]

Suggested inclusions for letters, notes, and conversations:

Scriptures:

Psalm 119:69

> Though the arrogant have smeared me with lies, I keep your precepts with all my heart.

Proverbs 12:19

> Truthful lips endure forever, but a lying tongue lasts only a moment.

Proverbs 15:1

> A gentle answer turns away wrath, but a harsh word stirs up anger.

Matthew 5:11

> Blessed are you when people insult you, persecute you and falsely say all kinds of evil against you because of me.

John 15:20

> Remember the words I spoke to you: 'No servant is greater than his master.' If they persecuted me, they will persecute you also. If they obeyed my teaching, they will obey yours also.

I Corinthians 4:13a

when we are slandered, we answer kindly

II Corinthians 4:8-9

8 We are hard pressed on every side, but not crushed; perplexed, but not in despair;
9 persecuted, but not abandoned; struck down, but not destroyed.

II Timothy 3:12

In fact, everyone who wants to live a godly life in Christ Jesus will be persecuted.

Words to say

- Listen to your heart.
- If there is no reason to believe what's been said, don't.
- Remember always that God knows the truth.
- We only have to answer for ourselves, our words, our actions.
- If you've been targeted because of your faith, rejoice!
- Be fair in what you say and do in return.
- Pray for those who have accused you.
- Love those who have done you wrong.

Words to pray—if you want to close your letter or conversation with a prayer, you might include:

- Prayer that God will soften the anger within the person's heart.
- Prayer that the person will refrain from retaliation.
- Praise to God for the righteousness of the offended.
- Prayer that broken relationships might be restored.
- Prayer that the person will stand firm in faith.

Summary

As you've read this handbook, perhaps you've thought of a friend or acquaintance who could use a word of encouragement right now. If so, then it's time to begin. Think of the positive repercussions your notes, phone calls, or face to face words of encouragement might have. As a pebble thrown into still water, your encouragement might cause a rippling effect, touching others, on and on.

Discouraged persons are all around — adults and children. Waiting to be picked up and lifted in spirit, they are weary and suffering. I'll add one final illustration:

Suffering comes to all of us, and no one can suffer for us. Even so, we can be supported in those difficult times by the prayers and understanding of loved ones and friends. It's when we are too proud to admit our need to others that we are in the greatest danger.

The Sequoia trees of California tower as much as 300 feet above the ground. Strangely, these giants have unusually shallow root systems that reach out in all directions to capture the greatest amount of surface moisture. Seldom will you see a redwood standing alone because high winds would quickly uproot it. That's why they grow in clusters. Their intertwining roots provide support for one another against the storms.

Support is what Jesus wanted from Peter, James, and John in Gethsemane as he faced Calvary. On the cross as the world's sin- bearer He would experience His Father's wrath and abandonment. That was the awful cup He prayed would be taken from Him. In that dark hour, He looked to His disciples for prayerful alertness and compassion. But oh, how they disappointed Him! Somehow the sight of His sleeping disciples must have made the isolation of Gethesemane that much more painful.

If Jesus looked to human support in His crisis hour, how much more do Christians need one another when they suffer! Let's be willing to ask someone to pray for us and with us. And let's be alert for opportunities to lend our support to others who are suffering. [2]

Our world needs encouragers more today than ever. And now, *you know what to say!*

Endnotes

[1] Taken from *ENCOURAGE ME* by Charles Swindoll. Copyright©1982 by Charles R. Swindoll, Inc. Used by permission of Zondervan Publishing House.

[2] Reprinted by permission from Parsons Technology, One Parsons Drive, Hiawatha, IA 52233, *Bible Illustrator* software.

[3] Bob Slosser, *Miracle in Darien* (Plainfield, NJ: Logos International, 1979), p. 198.